Report to Congressional Committees

I0426051

March 2012

EXPORT CONTROLS

Proposed Reforms Create Opportunities to Address Enforcement Challenges

GAO

Accountability ★ Integrity ★ Reliability

GAO-12-246

Highlights

Highlights of GAO-12-246, a report to congressional committees

EXPORT CONTROLS

Proposed Reforms Create Opportunities to Address Enforcement Challenges

Why GAO Did This Study

The U.S. government controls the export of sensitive defense and dual-use items (having both military and commercial use). The five agencies primarily responsible for export control enforcement—the Departments of Commerce, Homeland Security (DHS), Justice, State and the Treasury—conduct inspections and investigations, and can levy punitive actions against violators. A challenging aspect of export control enforcement is the detection of illicit transshipments—the transfer of items from place of origin through an intermediary country to an unauthorized destination, such as Iran. In 2010, the President announced reforms to the U.S. export control system to address weaknesses found by GAO and others. GAO was asked to address how the export control enforcement agencies allocate resources, as well as the challenges they face and the potential impact of export control reform on enforcement activities. GAO reviewed documents and met with enforcement agency officials as well as with U.S. and foreign government and company officials in Hong Kong, Singapore, and the United Arab Emirates, which have a high volume of trade and have been identified as potential hubs for illicit transshipments.

What GAO Recommends

GAO recommends that Commerce, DHS, Justice, and State take steps individually and with other agencies through the national Export Enforcement Coordination Center to better manage export control enforcement resources and improve the license determination process. Agencies agreed with GAO's recommendations.

View GAO-12-246. For more information, contact Belva Martin at (202) 512-4841 or martinb@gao.gov.

What GAO Found

Agencies use a risk-based approach, including workload and threat assessment data, to allocate resources, but most do not fully track those used for export control enforcement activities. As their missions are broader than export controls, agencies can use staff resources for other activities based on need, making tracking resources used solely for export control enforcement difficult. Only Commerce's Office of Export Enforcement allocates its resources exclusively to export control enforcement as that is its primary mission. Other agencies, such as State and the Treasury, have relatively few export control enforcement staff to track. While several agencies acknowledge the need to better track export enforcement resources and have taken steps to do so, they do not know the full extent of their use of these resources and do not use this information in resource allocation decisions. In some cities, agencies are informally leveraging export enforcement resources through voluntarily created local task forces that bring together enforcement resources to work collectively on export control cases.

Enforcement agencies face several challenges in investigating illicit transshipments, both domestically and overseas, which potentially reduce the effectiveness of enforcement activities and limit the identification and investigation of illicit transshipments. These include:

- *License Determination Delays*. License determinations—which confirm whether an item is controlled and requires a license, and thereby help confirm whether an export control violation has occurred—are often not timely, potentially hindering investigations and prosecutions.
- *Limited Secure Communications and Cleared Staff*. Investigators have limited access to secure communications and staff with high-level security clearances in several domestic field offices, limiting investigators' ability to share timely and important information.
- *Lack of Trend Data on Illicit Transshipments*. While there is a good exchange of intelligence between enforcement agencies and the intelligence community—to seize shipments and take other actions against export control violators—officials noted that no formal process or means existed for these groups to collectively quantify and identify statistical trends and patterns relating to information on illicit transshipments.
- *Lack of Effectiveness Measures Unique to the Complexity of Export Controls*. Investigative agencies lack measures of effectiveness that fully reflect the complexity and qualitative benefits of export control cases.

Some of these challenges may be addressed by ongoing export control reform initiatives, but reform presents both opportunities and challenges. Revising the control list could simplify the license determination process, but could also result in the need for increased enforcement activity overseas to validate the recipient of the items as fewer items may require U.S. government approval in advance of shipment. As most staff located overseas have other agency and mission-related priorities, their availability may be limited. The newly created national Export Enforcement Coordination Center is intended to help agencies coordinate their export control enforcement efforts as well as share intelligence and law enforcement information related to these efforts. However, it is unclear whether the center will address all of the challenges GAO found, as detailed plans for its operations are under development.

_____ **United States Government Accountability Office**

Contents

Figure

Abbreviations

AECA	Arms Export Control Act
CBP	Customs and Border Protection
DDTC	Directorate of Defense Trade Controls
DHS	Department of Homeland Security
DOD	Department of Defense
DTSA	Defense Technology Security Administration
EAA	Export Administration Act
EAGLE	Export and Anti-proliferation Global Law Enforcement
FBI	Federal Bureau of Investigation
GPRA	Government Performance Results Act
ICE	Immigration and Customs Enforcement
OEE	Office of Export Enforcement
OFAC	Office of Foreign Assets Control
UAE	United Arab Emirates

United States Government Accountability Office
Washington, DC 20548

March 27, 2012

The Honorable Susan M. Collins
Ranking Member
Committee on Homeland Security and Governmental Affairs
United States Senate

The Honorable Jon Kyl
Ranking Member
Subcommittee on Crime and Terrorism
Committee on the Judiciary
United States Senate

Each year, billions of dollars in defense and "dual-use" items—items that have both commercial and military applications—are exported to U.S. allies and strategic partners to further national security, foreign policy, and economic interests.[1] The U.S. government protects these items through its export control system to ensure that they are transferred to foreign parties in a manner consistent with U.S. interests. The current system is governed by a complex set of laws, regulations, and processes and is implemented by multiple agencies, some with overlapping jurisdiction. Enforcement, a key function in the system, strives to prevent or deter the illegal export of defense and dual-use items such as controlled components that were shipped to countries like Iran, which were later found in weapons and devices used against U.S. forces in Iraq. Export control enforcement activities include inspecting items to be exported, investigating potential export control violations, and pursuing and imposing criminal and administrative penalties against violators. These activities also seek to keep defense and dual-use items from being illicitly transshipped through intermediary countries or locations, such as the United Arab Emirates (UAE), Hong Kong,[2] Singapore, and Malaysia, where a high volume of trade provides potential opportunities for the illicit transshipment of export-controlled items to an unauthorized final

---

[1]For the purposes of this report, the term defense items refers to defense articles, defense services, and related technical data, as specified in 22 U.S.C. § 2778, and the term dual-use refers to items that have both commercial and military applications, such as computers, radars, and telecommunication equipment.

[2]Hong Kong is a special administrative region of China.

destination, such as Iran.[3] For the purposes of this report, illicit transshipment is the transfer of merchandise from its place of origin through an intermediary country to an unauthorized destination. For example, in September 2011, a Pakistani citizen pleaded guilty to conspiring to commit export violations in connection with a scheme to illegally export U.S. nuclear-related materials, by exporting these materials from the United States through the UAE, to several restricted entities in Pakistan. The Department of State and other federal agencies have recognized illicit transshipment as a major weakness in trade and national security.

In 2006, we found that U.S. export control enforcement agencies faced considerable challenges and made several recommendations to improve interagency coordination, and we continue to include the U.S. export control system as a key component of a GAO high risk area on protecting technologies critical to U.S. national security interests.[4] Noting challenges in the entire U.S. export control system, in April 2010, the President announced a reform strategy that included the creation of a single export enforcement coordination agency as a primary forum where agencies can coordinate and enhance export control enforcement efforts and resolve conflicts. However, some members of Congress have raised questions about existing export control activities including resources agencies are devoting to these activities. Moreover, they have expressed concerns that without addressing existing enforcement problems, reform of the export control system could exacerbate current shortfalls in the system designed to prevent countries and entities of concern from obtaining sensitive U.S. defense and dual-use items. In response to your request, we identified (1) how agencies allocate staff resources for export control enforcement activities, and (2) challenges that agencies face in investigating illicit transshipments and the potential impact of export control reform initiatives on enforcement activities.

To conduct our work, we reviewed laws, regulations, and guidelines relating to the enforcement of U.S. export controls on defense and dual-

---

[3]U.S. exports to Iran, including defense and dual-use items are severely restricted by U.S. laws and regulations. Current sanctions on Iran, which are administered by the Department of the Treasury, ban almost all U.S. exports to that country.

[4]GAO, *Export Controls: Challenges Exist in Enforcement of an Inherently Complex System*, GAO-07-265 (Washington, D.C.: Dec. 20, 2006); and *GAO's 2011 High-Risk Series, An Update*, GAO-11-278 (Washington D.C.: Feb. 2011).

use items and interviewed officials from the Departments of Commerce, Defense (DOD), Homeland Security (DHS), Justice, State, and the Treasury as well as private industry and foreign government officials. We also visited agency headquarters as well as three domestic and three international locations to obtain and analyze information on resources, knowledge of illicit transshipments, and challenges in investigating export controls for criminal violations. We corroborated information on resources with agency budget and other documents where possible. The domestic locations, Baltimore, MD; Los Angeles, CA; and San Francisco, CA; represent one or more of the following: a large percentage of the investigative caseload, ports with a high volume of trade of U.S. commodities, and a large presence of aerospace, electronics, and software industries and geographic dispersion. The international locations, Hong Kong, Singapore, and the UAE, represent three of the top 10 ports in the world for trade volume and have been identified by federal agency officials as potential hubs for illicit transshipments of defense and dual-use items. We also met with cognizant agency officials to discuss progress, opportunities, and challenges of the President's current export control reform initiatives. (See appendix I for more details.)[5]

We conducted this performance audit from February 2011 through March 2012, in accordance with generally accepted government auditing standards. Those standards require that we plan and perform the audit to obtain sufficient, appropriate evidence to provide a reasonable basis for our findings and conclusions based on our audit objectives. We believe that the evidence obtained provides a reasonable basis for our findings and conclusions based on our audit objectives.

Background

The U.S. government's control over the export of defense and dual-use items is intended to ensure that U.S. interests are protected in accordance with the Arms Export Control Act (AECA) and the Export

---

[5]In March 2012, we reported on export control compliance and monitoring activities. However, the details were deemed sensitive, but unclassified by the agencies, and so are not described more fully in this report.

Administration Act (EAA).[6] Defense items can include tanks, fighter aircraft, submarines, firearms, satellites, missiles, and training; while dual-use items can include computers, radars, and telecommunication equipment. Jurisdiction over the export of defense and dual-use items is primarily divided between State and Commerce. Generally, unless an exemption applies, exporters submit a license application to State if their items are controlled on the U.S. Munitions List[7] or to Commerce if their items are controlled on the Commerce Control List pursuant to the Export Administration Regulations to receive export approval. As part of the application review process, State and Commerce consult with other departments, including DOD and with Treasury in the case of sanctioned countries. Offices within Commerce, DHS, Justice, and State conduct enforcement activities. Treasury and Commerce administer the current sanctions program for designated countries.

Export control enforcement actions consist of three primary functions—inspecting and seizing goods, investigating potential violators, and levying punitive actions against violators of export control laws.[8] As shown in table 1, these functions are largely conducted by various agencies within Commerce, DHS, Justice, State, and the Treasury depending on the facts and circumstances of the case.[9] Multiple laws, regulations, and directives provide differing enforcement authority for U.S. agencies to inspect,

---

[6]22 U.S.C. § §2751-2799aa-2 and 50 U.S.C. app. §§ 2401-2420. The Export Administration Act is not permanent legislation. 50 U.S.C. app. § 2419. Authority granted under the act lapsed in August 2001. However, Executive Order 13,222, Continuation of Export Control Regulations, which was issued in August 2001 under the authority provided by the International Emergency Economic Powers Act (50 U.S.C. §§ 1701-1707.), continues the controls established under the act, and the implementing Export Administration Regulations. Executive Order 13,222 requires an annual extension and was recently renewed by Presidential Notice on August 12, 2011. 76 Fed. Reg. 50,661 (Aug. 16, 2011).

[7]U.S. defense items are also sold and exported to foreign governments through the U.S. government's Foreign Military Sales program.

[8]Actions can also include compliance and monitoring, such as reviewing disclosures by exporters of possible export control violations, prelicense checks, and postshipment verifications. See GAO, *Export Controls: Post-Shipment Verification Provides Limited Assurance That Dual-use Items Are Being Properly Used*, GAO-04-357 (Washington, D.C.: Jan. 12, 2004); and *Defense Trade: Arms Export Control System in the Post 9/11 Environment*, GAO-05-234 (Washington, D.C.: Feb. 16, 2005).

[9]Other departments, including Defense and Energy, may provide technical expertise on items to enforcement agencies. Also, Defense and the military services have investigative units that may provide support to the enforcement agencies.

investigate, and take punitive action against potential violators of U.S. export control laws. These authorities provide the Federal Bureau of Investigation (FBI) and Immigration and customs Enforcement (ICE) with overlapping jurisdiction to investigate defense potential violations, and FBI, ICE, and Commerce's Office of Export Enforcement (OEE) with overlapping jurisdiction to investigate dual-use potential violations.

Table 1: Export Control Enforcement Activities, by Departments and Agency

	Inspection[a]	Investigation	Punitive action[b]
Commerce			
Bureau of Industry and Security Office of Chief Counsel			●
Office of Export Enforcement (OEE)P[c]		●	
DHS			
U.S. Customs and Border Protection (CBP)	●		●[d]
U.S. Immigration and Customs Enforcement (ICE)		●	
Justice			
U.S. Attorneys' Offices			●
Federal Bureau of Investigation (FBI)		●	
State			
Directorate of Defense Trade Controls (DDTC)			●
Office of Legal Adviser for Political-Military Affairs			●
Treasury			
Office of Foreign Assets Control (OFAC)			●

Source: GAO analysis of information provided by each agency and export control laws and regulations.

[a]CBP and ICE both have the authority to conduct inspections at U.S. ports, but, according to CBP officials, CBP has a primary role in this area.

[b]For purposes of this report, punitive actions can be either criminal or administrative against potential violators of export control laws and regulations. Criminal actions taken against violators of export control laws and regulations can result in imprisonment, fines, forfeitures, and other penalties. Administrative actions against violators can include fines, suspension of an export license, or denial or debarment from exporting.

[c]Commerce's Office of Enforcement Analysis provides analytic support to OEE.

[d]CBP can seize items being exported contrary to law, including those subject to export controls, and can also issue penalties under the Foreign Trade Regulations for false or fraudulent reporting on or misuse of the Automated Export System.

Inspections of items scheduled for export are routinely conducted at U.S. air, sea, and land ports, as part of the U.S. Customs and Border

Protection (CBP) officer's responsibilities for enforcing U.S. import and export control laws and regulations at our nation's ports of entry. CBP's enforcement activities include inspection of outbound cargo through a risk-based approach using CBP's automated targeting systems to assess the risk of each shipment, review and validation of documentation presented for licensable items, detention of questionable shipments, and seizure of shipments and issuance of monetary penalties for items that are found to be in violation of U.S. export control laws.[10] According to CBP officials, almost 3 million shipments per month are exported from the United States.

Investigations of potential violations of export control laws for dual-use items are conducted by agents from OEE, ICE, and FBI. Investigations of potential export control violations involving defense items are conducted by ICE and FBI agents. OEE and ICE are authorized to investigate potential violations of dual-use items. ICE is also authorized to investigate potential violations of defense items. The FBI has authority to investigate any criminal violation of law not exclusively assigned to another agency, and is mandated to investigate and oversee export control violations with a counterintelligence concern. The investigative agencies have various tools for investigating potential violations (see table 2) and establishing cases for potential criminal or administrative punitive actions.

---

[10]According to CBP officials it refers most export seizures to ICE for potential case development, including information on all shipments where weapons are involved or CBP officers have some reason to believe there is a potential for criminal activity. A number of these referrals lead to ICE investigations.

Table 2: Key Investigative Tools for Investigative Export Control Enforcement Activities

Investigative tool	OEE[a]	ICE	FBI
Undercover operations	✓	✓	✓
Searches without warrants at the borders		✓	
Wiretaps	✓	✓	✓
Overseas investigations[b]	✓	✓	✓
Access and use of forfeiture funds	✓	✓	✓

Source: GAO analysis of export control laws and regulations and information provided by the agencies.

[a] While OEE conducts short-term undercover operations, it does not have independent authority to use nonappropriated funds to finance such operations or to operate undercover proprietorships. According to OEE, it is seeking additional statutory authorities in the areas of overseas investigations, undercover operations, forfeiture authority, and wiretapping authority.

[b] Enforcement agencies can conduct overseas investigations with host government concurrence.

Punitive actions, which are either criminal or administrative, are taken against violators of export control laws and regulations, and may involve U.S. or foreign individuals and companies. Criminal violations are those cases where the evidence shows that the exporter willfully violated export control laws. U.S. Attorneys' Offices prosecute export control enforcement criminal cases in consultation with Justice's National Security Division. These cases can result in imprisonment, fines, forfeitures, and other penalties. Punitive actions for administrative violations can include fines, suspension of an export license, or denial or debarment from exporting, and are imposed primarily by State or Commerce, depending on whether the violation involves the export of a defense or a dual-use item. For example, Commerce can impose the administrative sanction of placing parties acting contrary to the national security or foreign policy interests of the United State on a list that prevents their receipt of items subject to Commerce controls. The Treasury's Office of Foreign Assets Control (OFAC) administers and enforces economic sanctions programs primarily against countries and groups of individuals, such as terrorists and narcotics traffickers. The sanctions can be either comprehensive or selective, using the blocking of assets and trade restrictions to accomplish foreign policy and national security goals. In some cases, both criminal and administrative penalties can be levied against an export control violator. In fiscal year 2010, Justice data showed that 56 individuals or companies were convicted of criminal violations of export control laws.[11] State reported over $43 million and Commerce reported more than $25.4 million in administrative fines and penalties for fiscal year 2010. In 2011, over a third of the major U.S. export control enforcement and embargo-related criminal prosecutions involved the illegal transfer of U.S. military, nuclear, or technical data to Iran and China.

Agencies Use a Risk-Based Approach to Allocate Resources but Do Not Fully Track Those Used For Export Control Enforcement

Agencies use some form of a risk-based approach when allocating resources to export control enforcement as their missions are broader than export controls. As agencies can use these resources for other activities based on need, tracking resources used solely on export control enforcement activities is difficult. Only OEE allocates all of its resources exclusively to export control enforcement as that is its primary mission, and State and the Treasury have relatively few export control enforcement staff to track. Agencies' risk-based resource allocation approach incorporates a variety of information, including workload and threat assessment data, but has not generally included data on resources used for export control enforcement activities as agencies did not implement systems to fully track this information until recently. Given the overlapping jurisdiction of several enforcement agencies, in some cities agencies have voluntarily created local task forces that bring together enforcement resources to work collectively on cases—informally leveraging resources.

Most Agencies—Whose Missions Are Broader Than Export Controls—Have Limited Data on Resources Used for Export Control Enforcement

Agencies determine their missions based on statutes, policy, and directives, and articulate their fundamental mission in their strategic plans.[12] Based on our review of these documents as well as discussions with senior agency officials, agencies with primary export control enforcement responsibility have multiple missions that extend beyond export controls as shown in table 3, except for OEE. As such, these agencies are faced with balancing multiple priorities when allocating staff resources.

---

[11]Data provided by Justice for criminal convictions where 50 U.S.C. § 1705 or 22 U.S.C. § 2778 was charged.

[12]A strategic plan, according to the Government Performance and Results Act (as amended), articulates, among other things, the major functions and operations of an organization, and describes its long-term general goals for implementing those functions or operations, including the resources needed to reach these goals.

Table 3: Primary Missions of the Agencies with Export Control Enforcement Responsibility

Department/agency	Mission
Commerce	
• OEE	Investigate potential violations of dual-use and commercial exports with a priority related to weapons of mass destruction, terrorism, and unauthorized military use.
DHS	
• CBP	Detect and prevent terrorist and terrorist weapons from entering U.S. ports, and inspecting items and persons entering and leaving the United States.
• ICE	Investigate drug smuggling, human trafficking and smuggling, financial crimes, commercial fraud, intellectual property rights violations, document fraud, money laundering, child exploitation, immigration fraud, and potential defense and dual-use export violations.
Justice	
• U.S. Attorneys' Office	Prosecute violations of federal criminal laws and litigate civil matters on behalf of the United States. Criminal prosecutions include cases involving terrorism, counterterrorism, government contractor fraud, and many others.
• FBI	Protect the United States against terrorist and foreign intelligence threats and enforce criminal laws.
• National Security Division	Supports export control enforcement through its technical expertise to prosecutors and law enforcement agencies.
State	
• DDTC	Control the export and temporary import of defense articles and defense services covered by the United States Munitions List and brokering activities by U.S. and foreign persons.
Treasury	
• OFAC	Administer and enforce economic and trade sanctions based on US foreign policy and national security goals against targeted foreign countries and regimes, terrorists, international narcotics traffickers, those engaged in activities related to the proliferation of weapons of mass destruction, and other threats to the national security, foreign policy or economy of the United States.

Source: GAO analysis of agency information.

The agencies with export control enforcement responsibilities use some form of a risk-based approach to allocate staff resources, but several agencies, including CBP, FBI, ICE, and the U.S. Attorneys' Offices, did not implement systems to fully track the staff time spent on enforcement activities until recently. Only OEE allocates its entire investigative staff to this mission. As most enforcement resources are used to enforce a wide variety of laws, not just export control laws, if an important need arises, enforcement agencies have the flexibility to use these resources for other, non-export control related duties. Table 4 shows the total domestic staff, by agency that was allocated to conduct export control enforcement activities in fiscal year 2010. The number of officers, agents, and investigators who actually work on export control enforcement may be less than the number allocated for each agency.

Table 4: Enforcement Agency Total Staff and Staff Allocated for Domestic Export Control Enforcement, Fiscal Year 2010

Agency	Total staff	Staff allocated for export control enforcement
Commerce: OEE	109 investigators	95 investigators[a]
DHS: CBP	20,455 officers	658 officers[b]
DHS: ICE/Homeland Security Investigations	6,700 investigators	Data not publicly available
Justice: FBI[c]	12,092 agents	Data not publicly available
Justice: U.S. Attorneys[d]	4,005 criminal attorneys	292 criminal attorneys[e]
State: DDTC	21 specialists	10 specialists
State: Office of Legal Adviser for Political-Military Affairs	12 attorneys	1 attorney
Commerce: Office of the Chief Counsel, Bureau of Industry and Security	12 attorneys	9 attorneys
Treasury: OFAC	27 enforcement officers	None

Source: GAO analysis of agency information.

[a]All investigators are used solely for export control enforcement activities and, according to Commerce, an additional 39 staff are available to provide analytic support.

[b]CBP officers conduct outbound enforcement activities which include both the passenger and cargo environments.

[c]FBI agents are not used solely for export control enforcement activities, but generally handle these cases through their Counterintelligence Division. The resources that FBI uses for these activities are classified.

[d]U.S. Attorneys are not used solely for export control enforcement activities.

[e]This figure represents the number of attorneys who have been specially allocated to work on terrorism and national security cases, which includes but is not limited to export enforcement cases.

These agencies have systems to track staff resources used for their primary missions and several have acknowledged the need to better track export control enforcement resources and have taken steps to do so. The Government Performance and Results Act (GPRA) of 1993 laid the foundation for results-oriented agency planning, measurement, and reporting in the federal government, highlighting the important role performance information plays in improving the efficiency and effectiveness of an agency.[13] The GPRA Modernization Act of 2010

---

[13] Pub. L. No. 103-62.

reinforces these principles.[14] One key element of these principles includes having accurate data agencies can use to allocate resources, among other things.[15] However, most of the agencies responsible for inspecting, investigating, and prosecuting potential export control violations did not know the full extent of the use of staff resources on these activities, and as such, have not used this information in resource allocation decisions, as outlined in the examples below.

- OEE allocates all of its investigators solely to export control enforcement, and as such, is the only agency that has been able to fully track the resources used on these activities. To formulate its budget and allocate its investigators, OEE conducts threat assessments with a priority related to weapons of mass destruction, terrorism, and unauthorized military use; and analyzes export control enforcement case workload, including the prior year's investigative statistics of arrests, indictments, and convictions. OEE also recently completed a field office expansion study to decide which cities would be the best locations for additional OEE field offices. In this study, OEE considered the volume of licensed and unlicensed exports and the type of high-tech items exported from different areas of the United States, and concluded that Atlanta, GA; Cincinnati, OH; Phoenix, AZ; and Portland, OR, were optimal locations, but has not received budget approval for expansion.
- CBP reemphasized outbound operations in the creation of its Outbound Enforcement Division in March 2009 to help prevent terrorist groups, rogue nations, and other criminal organizations from obtaining defense and dual-use commodities; enforce sanctions and trade embargoes; and increase exporter compliance. CBP determines the number of staff to allocate to outbound inspections through a risk-based approach based on prior workload and a quarterly threat matrix—which includes the volume of outbound cargo and passengers, port threat assessments, and the numbers and types of seizures and arrests at the ports for items such as firearms and currency. As of fiscal year 2010, CBP had allocated approximately 660 officers for outbound enforcement activities, but these officers can be used for other than export control-related activities at any time,

---

[14]Pub. L. No. 111-352 (2011).

[15]GAO, *National Export Initiative: U.S. and Foreign Commercial Service Should Improve Performance and Resource Allocation Management*, GAO-11-909 (Washington, D.C.: Sept. 29, 2011).

when needed. For example, the Port of Baltimore has officers assigned to perform outbound activities at both the airport and seaport, some of which focus on the enforcement of controlled shipments in the seaport environment. According to the Port Director, any of these officers can be redirected at any time and often are assigned to the airport during the busy airline arrival times, to perform inbound inspection duties—based on priorities. Further, CBP does not track the hours that its officers across the country spend on export control enforcement activities, but is in the process of implementing a system to do so. CBP officials stated that determining the right mix of officers is complex and changes to its tracking system should allow for better planning and accounting for resources used for outbound activities in the future.

- ICE's Homeland Security Investigations, Counter-Proliferation Investigations Unit focuses on preventing sensitive U.S. technologies and weapons from reaching the hands of adversaries and conducts export control investigations. To determine how many investigators it should allocate to this unit, ICE uses information including operational threat assessments and case data from the previous year, by field office, on total numbers of arrests, indictments, convictions, seizures, and investigative hours expended on export control investigations. For example, it assigns a tier level for each of its 70 field offices, based on threat assessments—ranging from 1 for the highest threat, resulting in a larger number of agents assigned to these offices; to 5 for the lowest threat, with a lower number of agents assigned. To further prioritize resources, in 2010, ICE established Counter Proliferation Investigations Centers in selected cities throughout the United States, with staff focused solely on combating illegal exports and illicit procurement networks seeking to acquire vital U.S. technology. ICE concluded that it needed to form these centers to combat the specialized nature of complex export control cases and determined that its previous method of distributing resources needed refinement, noting that some ICE field office managers had difficulty in balancing numerous competing programmatic priorities and initiatives. According to ICE officials, they plan to mitigate these concerns by having staff and facilities focused solely on export control enforcement cases, which will allow ICE to track and use this information to better determine future resource needs.

- The FBI, with both an investigative and intelligence mission, does not allocate resources solely for export control enforcement and officials told us they view these activities as a tool to gain intelligence that may lead to more robust cases. Nevertheless, cases involving export controls are primarily led by agents within the Counterintelligence Division. To determine the number of agents to allocate to this division, the FBI uses a risk management process and threat assessments. Several years ago, the FBI established at least one Counterintelligence squad in each of its 56 field offices. In July 2011, the FBI established a Counterproliferation Center, merging its Counterintelligence Division and its Weapons of Mass Destruction Directorate to better focus their efforts and resources. The FBI is in the process of implementing new codes within its resource tracking system to obtain better information on agents' distribution of work, which will include time spent on investigations of defense and dual-use items.

- U.S. Attorneys' Offices have discretion to determine the resources that they will allocate to export control enforcement cases, based on national priorities and the individual priorities of the 94 districts. These priorities include law enforcement concerns for their district and leads from investigative agencies. In response to the risk associated with national security, which includes export control enforcement cases, staffing for national security activities has increased and several districts have created national security sections within their office. In 2008, the Executive Office for U.S. Attorneys provided codes for charging time and labeling cases to obtain better information on the U.S. Attorneys' Office distribution of work and those resources used for export control enforcement. However, some Assistant U.S. Attorneys told us that the time-keeping system is complicated as there are multiple codes and sub-categories in the tracking system and determining the correct codes is often subjective, making it difficult to track time spent on export control enforcement cases. Senior agency officials acknowledged this concern and are working with the U.S. Attorneys' Offices to provide better guidance to improve the accuracy of attorney time charges.

- Other offices, such as State's Office of the Legal Adviser for Political-Military Affairs and Commerce's Office of the Chief Counsel for the Bureau of Industry and Security assist the enforcement agencies by providing legal support. For example, Commerce's Office of the Chief Counsel pursues administrative enforcement actions against individuals and entities, but also reviews and advises on OEE recommendations for other administrative actions, such as temporary denials of licenses. In addition, DDTC and OFAC pursue administrative enforcement actions against violators. For example, OFAC administers and enforces U.S. economic and trade sanctions against designated foreign countries. While not all of staff in these offices are allocated to export control enforcement, these offices have relatively few staff to track.

In addition to a domestic presence, most export control enforcement agencies also allocate resources overseas, but only Commerce allocates resources exclusively to export control enforcement. For example, Commerce maintains Export Control Officers in six locations abroad; Beijing and Hong Kong, China; Abu Dhabi, UAE; New Delhi, India; Moscow, Russia; and Singapore, to support its dual-use export control enforcement activities. Given that these officers have regional responsibilities, they cover additional locations. For example, the Export Control Officer assigned to Singapore also covers Malaysia and Indonesia. While other agencies have field locations in many overseas locations, these resources are to support the agencies' broader missions and can be used for other duties based on the overseas mission priorities. For example, ICE has 70 offices in 47 foreign countries with more than 380 government and contract personnel which support all ICE enforcement activities, including export control. They can also be called upon to support various other DHS mission priorities. Specifically, the ICE agents we met with at the U.S. Embassy in Abu Dhabi also conduct activities in support of the full DHS mission and a great portion of their time is spent on visa security and a lesser amount on export control enforcement activities.

Agencies Informally Leverage Enforcement Resources through Local Task Forces

The export control enforcement investigative agencies often have offices located in the same cities or geographic areas. In many of these cities, agencies' officials said that they informally leverage each others' tools, authorities, and resources to coordinate investigations and share intelligence through local task forces allowing them to use resources more efficiently and avoid duplicating efforts or interfering with each other's cases. In 2007, Justice's National Export Enforcement Initiative encouraged local field offices with a significant export control threat to create task forces or other alternatives to coordinate enforcement efforts in their area. Since then, almost 20 U.S. Attorneys' Offices have created task forces of their own initiative or in conjunction with another enforcement agency, primarily in cities where these agencies are co-located to facilitate the investigation and prosecution of export control cases. Figure 1 shows the location of investigative agencies' major field offices, as well as the location of export control enforcement task forces.

Figure 1: Location of Export Control Enforcement Investigative Agency Major Field Offices and Task Forces (as of 2011)

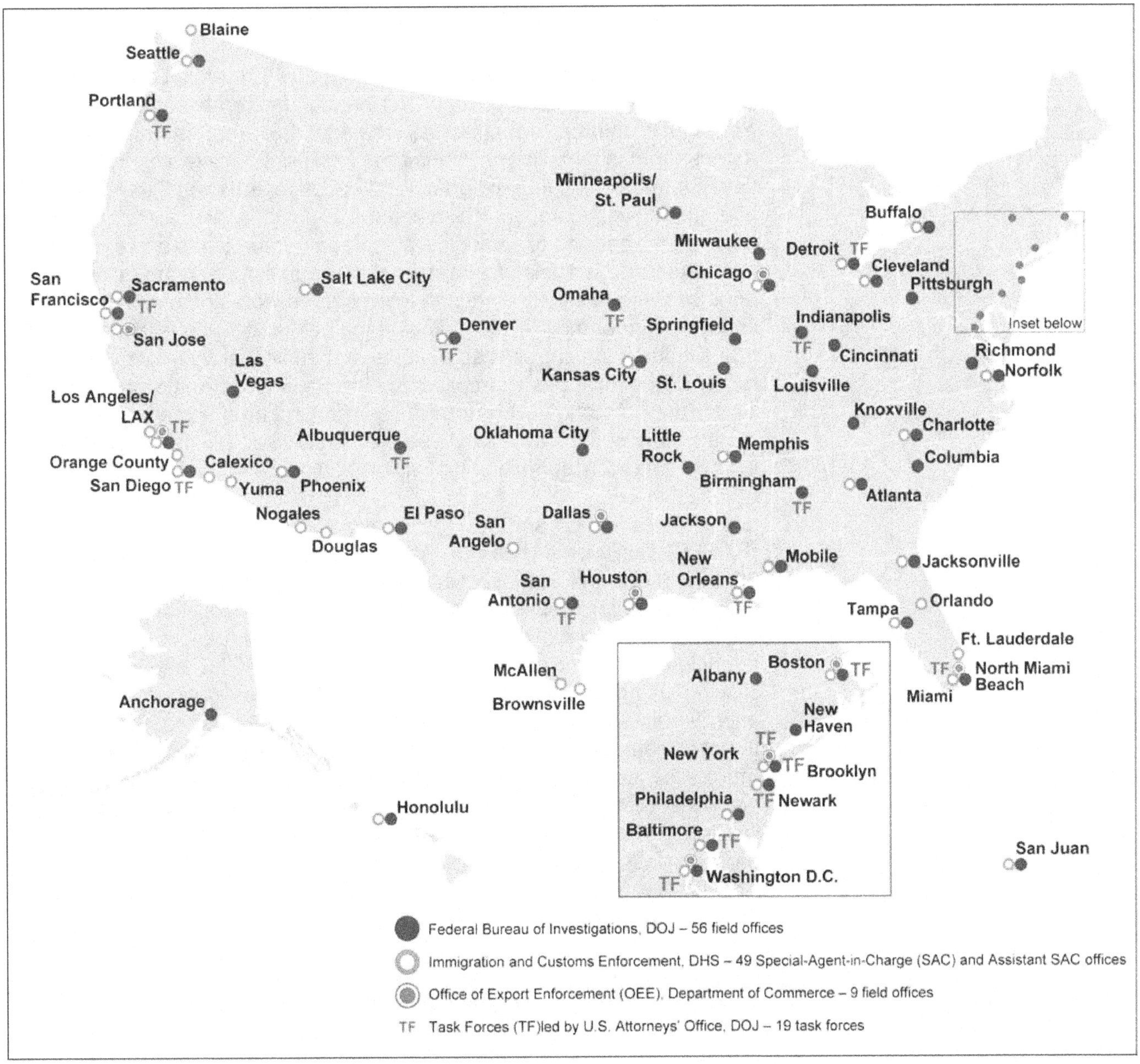

Federal Bureau of Investigations, DOJ – 56 field offices

Immigration and Customs Enforcement, DHS – 49 Special-Agent-in-Charge (SAC) and Assistant SAC offices

Office of Export Enforcement (OEE), Department of Commerce – 9 field offices

TF Task Forces (TF)led by U.S. Attorneys' Office, DOJ – 19 task forces

Source: GAO analysis of data provided by ICE, OEE, FBI, and the U.S. Attorneys' Office (data); Map Reserouces (map).

Most of the task force members we met with in Baltimore, Los Angeles, and San Francisco stated that they see benefits beyond the coordination of cases, including investigating cases together and sharing resources.

Baltimore's Counterproliferation Task Force: ICE and the U.S. Attorneys' Office created this Task Force in 2010 and it has representatives from each of the enforcement agencies located in the area, as well as the defense and intelligence communities. Task force officials stated that they develop and investigate export control cases together and, to enhance interagency collaboration, ICE has supplied work space, allowing agents from other agencies to work side-by-side to pursue leads and conduct investigations. Officials emphasized that the task force enables smaller agencies with fewer resources to leverage the work and expertise of the others to further their investigations and seek prosecutions. Sometimes the task force structures reap benefits that individual agencies cannot reach on their own, as exemplified by the Baltimore Counterproliferation Task Force. Among successes was a Maryland man sentenced to 8 months in prison followed by 3 years of supervised release for illegally exporting export-controlled night vision equipment.

Los Angeles' Export and Anti-proliferation Global Law Enforcement (EAGLE) Task Force: The U.S. Attorney established this Task Force in 2008 as a result of Justice's counter-proliferation initiatives. Its purpose is to coordinate and develop expertise in export control investigations. Currently, there are over 80 members from 17 Los Angeles-based federal agencies. According to a task force official, the EAGLE task force has resulted in increased priority on export control investigations and improved interagency cooperation since it was established. For instance, the enforcement agencies are now more effectively sharing information in their respective databases. A task force official noted that enhanced access to these databases allows agencies to reduce duplication of license determination requests and to easily retrieve information on a particular person or commodity's history using the search options. Additionally, through the task force structure, ICE and OEE agents have worked together to conduct additional outreach to industry affiliates.

San Francisco's Strategic Technology Task Force: According to officials, this task force was formed by FBI in 2004, with a primary focus on conducting joint export control outreach activities to academia and industry with the other investigative agencies (ICE and OEE). This task force also includes participation by the military service intelligence units and other law enforcement agencies. FBI task force leaders stated that this task force has helped to coordinate outreach activities as well as to generate investigative leads. According to an agent from the FBI's San Jose field office, that office has a performance goal to conduct 90 percent of their export control-related investigations jointly with investigative agencies at ICE and Commerce.

Although successful cases of joint collaboration among agencies can yield positive enforcement outcomes, as reported by the offices in the three cities we visited, the extent to which these alliances are effective is primarily dependent on personal dynamics of a given region, agency, and law enforcement culture. In addition, these local agency task forces for export control enforcement vary in structure, are voluntary, and do not exist nationwide. For example, while multiple investigative agencies have local offices in Chicago and Dallas with export control enforcement agents, agencies do not have a local task force in these cities to regularly coordinate on export control cases. While agency officials shared examples of agencies informally leveraging each other's resources, officials told us that they do not factor in such resources when planning their own agency allocations for a variety of reasons, including each agency's separate budgets and missions, which do not generally consider those of other agencies.

Reform Initiatives May Help Address Challenges In Investigating Illicit Transshipments But Detailed Plans Are Unknown

Enforcement agencies face several challenges in investigating illicit transshipments, both domestically and overseas—including license determination delays; limited access in some overseas locations; and a lack of effectiveness measures that reflect the complexity and qualitative benefits of export control cases. Recognizing broader challenges in export control enforcement, the President announced the creation of a national export enforcement coordination center, which may help agencies address some of the challenges described below, but detailed plans to do so have yet to be developed.

Investigators Face Several Challenges in Investigating Illicit Transshipments—Both Domestically and Overseas

The current export control enforcement system poses several challenges that potentially reduce the effectiveness of activities and limit the identification and investigation of illicit transshipments. Export control enforcement agencies seek to keep defense and dual-use items from being illegally exported through intermediary countries or locations to an unauthorized final destination, such as Iran, but agencies face challenges that can impact their ability to investigate export control violations, both domestically and overseas. First, license determinations—which confirm whether an item is controlled and requires a license, and thereby help confirm whether an export control violation has occurred—can sometimes be delayed, potentially hindering investigations and prosecutions. Second, investigators have limited access to secure communications and cleared staff in several domestic field offices, which can limit their ability to share timely and important information. Third, agencies have limited access to ports and facilities overseas. Fourth, agencies lack consistent data to quantify and identify trends and patterns in illicit transshipments of U.S. export-controlled items. Lastly, investigative agencies lack measures of effectiveness that fully reflect the complexity and qualitative benefits of export control cases.

License Determination Delays. To confirm whether a defense or dual-use item is controlled and requires a license, inspectors, investigators, and prosecutors request license determinations from the licensing agencies of State and Commerce.[16] These license determinations are integral to enforcement agencies' ability to seize items, pursue investigations, or seek prosecutions. DHS's Exodus Command Center operates the Exodus Accountability Referral System—an ICE database that initiates, tracks, and manages enforcement agency requests for license determinations from the licensing agencies.[17] Exodus Command Center guidance identifies three different levels of license determinations: initial (to seize an item or begin an investigation), pre-trial (to obtain a search warrant, among other things), and trial (to be used during trial proceedings). The Exodus Command Center has established internal timeliness goals for receiving responses to requests for initial determinations within 3 days; pre-trial certifications within 45 days; and trial certifications within 30 days. However, as shown in table 5, these goals are often not met, which can create barriers for enforcement agencies in seizing shipments before they depart the United States; obtaining search warrants; and making timely arrests.

---

[16]Depending on the license, the request can also go to Treasury's OFAC for sanctioned countries.

[17]The Exodus Command Center was established in 1982—and now is part of DHS/ICE—as the single point of contact for investigators and officers in the field needing operational support from export control agencies.

Table 5: Average License Determination Response Times (in Days)

License determination (goal)	Response time			
	FY 2007	FY 2008	FY 2009	FY 2010
Initial (3 days)				
- Defense items	8	5	7	10
- Dual-use items	19	19	23	30
Pre-Trial (45 days)				
- Defense items	126	91	64	93
- Dual-use items	10	18	29	81
Trial (30 days)				
- Defense items	N/A[a]	79	64	44
- Dual-use items	N/A[a]	N/A[a]	58	N/A[a]

Source: Data provided by the Exodus Command Center.
[a]Exodus Command Center officials noted that this information was not available.

According to State officials, they did not participate in developing the Exodus Command Center's goals, and State has different timeframes for responding to license determination requests. State officials noted that there is no statutory or regulatory requirement for the licensing agencies to provide license determinations and they must balance these activities with their primary mission of processing license applications. State officials told us their response to initial license determinations is a quick, unofficial assessment on whether or not an item is likely on the U.S. munitions list and it established a timeliness goal of 1-day to respond these requests. In 2004, State established a 30-day goal for responding to pre-trial and trial certification requests, but due to increased caseload and difficulty in meeting this goal, it revised it to 60-days. According to State officials, the number of requests from federal law enforcement for pre-trial and trial license determinations has increased significantly over the past 5 years—from 79 in fiscal year 2006 to 219 in fiscal year 2011, an increase of over 270 percent. Officials from State attribute some of the time it takes to process license determinations to the need to request interagency review and conduct additional analysis, as well as the complexity of the determination. For example, State sends all pre-trial and trial certification cases to DOD's Defense Technology Security Administration (DTSA) for its review, which can add to the time in responding to enforcement agencies' requests for license determinations. DTSA officials stated that these cases are reviewed through their normal licensing process and were not aware of any established timeframe goals, but stated that they expedite review of such license determination requests, for time-sensitive cases. As for complexity, according to State officials, those involving firearms, their components, and ammunition are relatively routine requests to respond to, whereas others involving multiple commodities, volumes of technical data, and complex services take more time and may involve multiple meetings and consultations among licensing agencies to make a determination. Further, State officials noted that they continue to educate law enforcement and work with ICE and FBI liaisons to ensure better information is provided in the request.

Commerce officials also noted that they did not participate in developing the Exodus Command Center's goals. Commerce has a 30-day goal for responding to initial license determination requests, but according to Commerce officials, does not have a specific timeframe for responding to pre-trial and trial certifications because they conduct an in-depth review in their initial determination. Commerce officials noted that they do not have a three-level system for processing license determinations and that it processes standard and certified license determination requests. While Commerce's standard determinations are equivalent to State's initial determinations, Commerce's approach differs from State's in that it conducts a more thorough review for this initial determination requiring more time than the 3-day goal established by the Exodus Command Center. Commerce's certified license determinations are equivalent to State's pre-trial and trial certifications, but these can take less time to complete if an initial determination was conducted. Commerce officials noted that, while they previously tracked and reported the timeliness of license determination requests in their annual reports, as of fiscal year 2011, they no longer track this information because they are generally able to process these in a timely manner based on the urgency of the request. Commerce officials also noted that the Exodus Command Center data on Commerce's response times do not reflect all license determinations, as OEE investigators request license determinations directly from Commerce licensing officers and FBI investigators can route such requests through OEE.

Limited Secure Communications and Cleared Staff. Limited access to secure communications, networks, facilities, and cleared staff by key investigative agencies including OEE and ICE can cause inconveniences and delays in the speed of export control investigations. While each of its field offices has access to secure telephones, none of the OEE field offices has its own secure networks or facilities—it accesses these through other agencies. According to some investigators that we spoke with, this limited access can sometimes create difficulties in communicating overseas, as well as working on cases jointly with the FBI.

This lack of immediate access to secure networks and facilities can limit investigators' ability to share timely and important information, according to agency officials. A field office agent from the FBI stated that the inability to fully communicate with investigators from other agencies can be challenging when working jointly on cases—including a lack of high-level security clearances that can be needed to discuss certain export control cases. According to OEE officials, they plan to equip each of their field offices with secure networks and facilities, and expect to complete installation of the secure networks during 2012. In addition, OEE is working to provide Top Secret-Sensitive Compartmented Information clearances to the remaining 37 of its 95 investigators that lack this clearance. According to ICE officials, most of the ICE field offices have access to secure telephones and data networks, but about half of these offices lack secure facilities and typically use those of other agencies, when needed.

Limited Overseas Access for Investigative Agencies. Enforcement agencies have differing levels of access to facilities and ports overseas when enforcing U.S. export control laws, which can limit their ability to carry out certain investigative activities. To pursue investigations of possible illicit transshipments, the U.S. government relies on the cooperation of host governments. According to agency officials, the success of enforcement activities abroad and the level of access granted is often determined by the U.S. government's relationship with the host government. For example, ICE in Abu Dhabi has fostered a relationship with the customs officials in the UAE and has worked with that government to create an academy and to provide UAE customs officials with various export control training sessions. According to the U.S. Deputy Chief of Mission and ICE attaché in the UAE, this collegial relationship has fostered better cooperation in several areas, including export controls. U.S. enforcement agencies overseas also rely on foreign counterparts to conduct enforcement activities. For example, the ICE attaché in Hong Kong told us that the Hong Kong government and its customs officials are helpful and responsive and that this relationship is further facilitated by the existence of a Customs Mutual Assistance Agreement, which allows direct contact and information exchange between U.S. and Hong Kong customs officials. In addition, Commerce has Export Control Officers stationed abroad and also has data sharing agreements with Hong Kong and Singapore to help ensure that U.S.-origin items are not retransferred without appropriate authorization. According to some State Department and agency officials overseas, while the existence of formal agreements with host governments, such as a Mutual Legal Assistance Treaty for prosecution or a Customs Mutual

Assistance Agreement allow for information sharing and assistance with the United States, these formal agreements do not guarantee that U.S. law enforcement will have access to foreign persons, ports, and facilities. Some agency officials overseas noted that such access is often dependent on the U.S. relationship with the host government regardless of the existence of formal agreements.

The lack of reciprocity in export control laws can also make it difficult to pursue export control violations abroad. The three key transshipment locations we visited, Hong Kong, Singapore, and the UAE each had their own national export control laws, and according to some State and overseas agency officials, these governments were most responsive to export control violations that fell under the international legal framework of United Nations' sanctions and major multilateral export control lists. Nevertheless, State officials noted that Hong Kong has had an extensive export and transshipment control system in place for over a decade. These officials also noted that they have identified and shared transshipment "best practices" that countries or locations can adopt to provide key legal authorities to better position them to enforce U.S. export control laws. In addition, investigators overseas told us that the lack of extradition treaties has limited their ability to pursue export control violators. The United States does not have an extradition treaty with the UAE, but it does have one with Hong Kong. While the United States has an extradition treaty with Singapore, it went into force over 70 years ago and, according to Singapore Embassy officials, it does not reflect current types of crimes and its renewal is unlikely. Despite these challenges, according to State, positive action relating to extradition has and continues to be achieved on a case-by-case basis.

Lack of Trend Data on Illicit Transshipments. No formal process exists between the investigative export control enforcement community and the intelligence community to share data or quantify and identify statistical trends and patterns relating to information on illicit transshipments. Although the total universe of items being illicitly transshipped is unknown, intelligence and law enforcement information is collected by the intelligence community, attaches in overseas posts, and the domestic export control enforcement agencies.[18] According to an OEE official,

---

[18]Transshipment can occur anywhere in the world, but is more likely to occur in ports with high volumes of trade activity.

there is a good exchange of actionable intelligence between the export control enforcement agencies and the intelligence community to seize shipments and take other actions against export control violators overseas. However, according to some enforcement and intelligence officials, intelligence leads are typically transmitted to either individual enforcement agencies or the enforcement community. Further, enforcement agencies maintain separate data related to their export control enforcement activities, which can include a variety of information such as shipment declarations listing countries of final destination and end-use or end-users and inspection and investigation results. Because the enforcement agencies have varying mission priorities in export controls, the availability and maintenance of data by the various agencies that can be used to identify illicit transshipments are not necessarily consistent or harmonized with each other.

Lack of Effectiveness Measures Unique to Complexity of Export Controls. The investigative enforcement agencies typically measure their effectiveness based on outcomes of enforcement activities, but these do not necessarily reflect the complexities involved with export control enforcement cases.[19] Specifically, ICE has a primary performance measure of the percentage of closed investigations that result in a law enforcement consequence—arrests, indictments, convictions, and seizures as shown in table 6.[20] OEE has similar enforcement metrics, and assesses impacts of their investigations by number of arrests, indictments, and convictions, as shown in table 7.[21] The numbers of arrests, indictments, and convictions for export control violation cases

---

[19]FBI is omitted as its measures of effectiveness include its intelligence function and these metrics are classified in nature.

[20]ICE now has a performance system that measures the percentage of high-impact or significant investigations that result in a transnational criminal disruption and/or dismantlement, and is applying this measure to its export control investigations. In addition, ICE is tracking systemic vulnerabilities nationally and within its respective field offices to prioritize efforts.

[21]OEE also measures effectiveness of headquarters' and field office performance and accomplishment on investigative actions that result in a prevention or deterrence of export violations; percentage of open cases focusing on OEE's export enforcement priorities; and administrative case results including the total dollar fines and other actions, such as denial orders.

have generally increased from fiscal years 2006 to 2010 for ICE and OEE.[22]

Table 6: ICE Number of Arrests, Indictments and Convictions for Defense and Dual-Use Items, Fiscal Years 2006 through 2010

Fiscal year	Arrests	Indictments	Convictions	Total
FY 2006	151	153	116	420
FY 2007	197	200	153	550
FY 2008	213	210	150	573
FY 2009	432	285	219	936
FY 2010	505	329	221	1055
Total	1498	1177	859	3534

Source: Data provided by ICE.

Table 7: OEE Number of Arrests, Indictments, and Convictions for Dual-Use Items, Fiscal Years 2006 through 2010

Fiscal year	Arrests	Indictments	Convictions	Total
FY 2006	11	17	36	64
FY 2007	26	17	16	59
FY 2008	20	57	40	117
FY 2009	37	69	33	139
FY 2010	22	62	31	115
Total	116	222	156	494

Source: Data provided by OEE.

While these numbers provide quantifiable performance assessments for the agencies' workload related to export control violations, they do not necessarily reflect the complex nature of these cases or measure agencies progress in achieving their goals. GPRA, as amended, requires federal agencies to develop performance measures to assess progress in achieving their goals and to communicate their availability to Congress. Under this act, agencies are to develop measures that are objective, quantifiable, measurable, and to establish performance measures that define the level of progress to be achieved using these goals. However,

---

[22]It is likely that the data provided by ICE in table 6 also include some of the same cases provided by OEE in table 7, thus may contain double-counting.

current measures used by the enforcement agencies do not fully capture these elements. According to ICE documentation, export control investigations often take an average of 2 to 3 years to complete, and although significant to national security, these investigations result in enforcement statistics that are low in comparison with other law enforcement disciplines. The performance measures used by ICE and OEE during the period of this review emphasized quantifiable outcomes of enforcement actions and they are working towards developing measures that take into account the length of time and effort for investigators to gather intelligence that could potentially reveal a larger group of violators and to collect evidence from a wide variety of sources, including those located overseas. Although quantitative law enforcement metrics may be useful for the enforcement community in understanding the volume of activities that investigative agencies are processing, they may encourage agents to pursue less significant investigations in order to meet these performance standards. Measuring arrests does not indicate success at impeding criminal operations or whether the vulnerabilities present within export control enforcement system have been minimized. While developing measures of effectiveness that adequately capture the time and resources spent on such activities as intelligence gathering may be difficult and not easily quantifiable failure to consider broader measures may run counter to the overall goal of preventing or deterring illegal exports. According to ICE officials, its new performance measures, as well as its system to measure and track vulnerabilities nationally and in its field locations, will improve its ability to measure outcomes of enforcement actions.

In 2010, we recommended that ICE establish performance measures for its investigative resources in a way to fully assess progress and better identify and decrease vulnerabilities.[23] ICE officials told us that they have made progress toward this goal by implementing new performance measures for investigations, including those relating to export control enforcement. For example, ICE in Los Angeles is in the process of creating performance measures which include: one or more arrests, indictments, convictions and/or quantifiable disruption of an illicit procurement network in defense and dual-use items. It also plans to factor in special interest countries known to contain entities that post a

---

[23]In September 2010, we reported on ICE's allocation of investigative resources. However, the details were deemed sensitive, but unclassified, by the agency, and so are not described more fully in this report.

credible public safety or national security threat, and have determined ten country destination codes that will be counted in measuring performance of its export control investigations.

Reform Initiatives Offer Opportunities to Address Some Export Control Enforcement Challenges but May Present Others

Our past work highlighted the need for export control reform. Over the past 10 years, we issued 22 reports with key findings and recommendations directed at State, Commerce, DOD, DHS, Justice, and Treasury, to improve the U.S. export control system, including enforcement activities.[24] In April 2010, the President announced a reform initiative to strengthen and streamline U.S. export controls by creating a single control list, licensing agency, information technology system, and enforcement coordination agency, aimed at addressing weaknesses in the system. The President is in the process of implementing several reform efforts. To coordinate export control enforcement activities, given that agencies have overlapping and duplicative authorities, in November 2010, the President announced the formation of a federal Export Enforcement Coordination Center to be established within DHS for administrative purposes. The corresponding Executive Order stated that to enhance enforcement efforts and minimize enforcement conflicts, executive departments and agencies must coordinate their efforts to detect, prevent, disrupt, investigate, and prosecute violations of U.S. export control laws, and must share intelligence and law enforcement information related to these efforts to the maximum extent possible consistent with national security and applicable law.[25] The Export Enforcement Coordination Center, which became operational in March 2012, is to:

- serve as the primary forum within the federal government for executive departments and agencies to coordinate and enhance their export control enforcement efforts and identify and resolve conflicts that have not been otherwise resolved in criminal and administrative investigations and actions involving violations of U.S. export control laws;

---

[24]GAO, *Export Controls: Agency Actions and Proposed Reform Initiatives May Address Previously Identified Weaknesses, but Challenges Remain*, GAO-11-135R (Washington, D.C.: Nov. 16, 2010).

[25]Exec. Order No.13,558, 75 Fed. Reg. 69,573 (Nov. 9, 2010).

- serve as a conduit between federal law enforcement agencies and the U.S. intelligence community for the exchange of information related to potential U.S. export control violations;
- serve as a primary point of contact between enforcement authorities and agencies engaged in export licensing;
- coordinate law enforcement public outreach activities related to U.S. export controls; and
- establish government-wide statistical tracking capabilities for U.S. criminal and administrative export control enforcement activities, to be conducted by DHS with information provided by and shared with all relevant departments and agencies participating in the center.

To date, a Director from ICE and Deputy Directors from the FBI and OEE have been appointed to lead the Export Enforcement Coordination Center and FBI, ICE, and OEE officials stated that they have agreed to a general interagency Concept of Operations, and are in the process of developing standard operating procedures. However, the center opened in March 2012—a delay of 9 months due to problems with completing the building on time as well as some difficulty in reaching interagency agreement on the Concept of Operations.

While the center may improve agency coordination, it is unclear whether it will address some of the specific challenges in investigating export control cases and illicit transshipments, as identified in this report. In our recently issued overview of government performance issues, we noted that many federal program efforts generally require the effective collaboration of more than one agency and that the GPRA Modernization Act of 2010 calls for a more coordinated and crosscutting approach, using outcome-oriented goals to identify and reduce unnecessary duplication, overlap, and fragmentation.[26] GPRA requires each agency to submit a strategic plan at least every 4 years, to include a description of how the agency is working with other agencies to achieve its strategic goals as well as the strategies to be used and resources needed to achieve these goals. However, it is not clear to what extent the Export Enforcement Coordination Center will coordinate efforts to increase efficiencies across enforcement agencies. In November 2010, we reported that co-location of the export control agencies in a single headquarters'-based facility may

---

[26]GAO, *Managing for Results: Opportunities for Congress to Address Government Performance Issues*, GAO-12-215R (Washington, D.C.: Dec. 9, 2011).

help agencies share information, but further action may be needed to fully coordinate export control enforcement cases throughout the country.[27] For example, agencies are unsure whether the center's yet-to-be-developed standard operating procedures will encourage enforcement agencies to fully leverage resources, as local level offices are informally doing in some cities, or develop combined measures of effectiveness for export control enforcement.

In addition, the Export Enforcement Coordination Center is to serve as a conduit between federal law enforcement agencies and the U.S. intelligence community. As noted in this report, no formal process or means exists between the investigative export control enforcement community and the intelligence community to quantify and identify statistical trends and patterns relating to information on illicit transshipments. While one of the goals of the center is to facilitate intelligence sharing, it has not yet been determined if this sharing of intelligence will go beyond specific investigative leads to obtain better information on trends and patterns relating to illicit transshipments of U.S. export-controlled items. However, an intelligence community liaison will be assigned to the center, which may allow for a better exchange of information between the enforcement and intelligence communities.

Beyond the creation of the Export Enforcement Coordination Center, other reforms are underway which could impact enforcement. As many of these reforms are in their infancy and detailed plans have not been released, enforcement agency officials shared their views that the planned reform initiatives for export control enforcement present both opportunities and challenges. For example, we also reported in November 2010, that one of the reform initiatives involves major revisions to the Commerce and State lists of dual-use and defense items that are controlled for export from the United States. This initiative was intended to clarify regulations for companies seeking to export arms and dual-use items to more easily determine whether items are regulated by State or Commerce. According to a State Department official, the revision of the control lists and the goal of clearer adjudication of the items controlled could reduce the time required to review the license determinations—allowing investigators to better focus their limited resources on those items critical to national security. However, as we previously reported, the

---

[27] GAO-11-135R.

review and possible removal of items controlled under the arms control list is taking longer than the agencies had originally anticipated. Some enforcement agency officials have raised concerns about changes to the control list, believing that as the U.S. Munitions List and Commerce Control List are revised, it could result in a decreased visibility of exports, requiring increased targeting by CBP to inspect items before they are exported overseas. Agency officials also stated that, as a result, increased enforcement activities may be needed overseas to validate the recipient of the item as fewer items would need U.S. government approval in advance of shipment.[28] As staff located overseas have other agency and mission-related priorities, their availability for increased enforcement and compliance activities may be limited. Commerce officials stated that their Export Control Officers stationed abroad allows them to dedicate resources to providing compliance and investigative activities for items impacted by export control reform. In addition, staffing changes may require an approval process involving the agency, State Department, and the Chief of Mission.[29] Also, some of the U.S. Attorneys we met with were concerned about the possible lack of a license with reform efforts, which they indicated is often relied upon in court to meet the high standards of evidence needed to prosecute export control cases. Other U.S. Attorneys stated that they were not as concerned, noting that cases involving non-licensable items have been successfully prosecuted. Further, as major changes to the State and Commerce control lists are made, investigators may need to increase outreach efforts to companies to provide education on U.S. export control laws. Specifically, in its fiscal year 2011 Performance and Accountability Report, Commerce stated that it will need to increase its outreach efforts to educate exporters about changes in export control regulations and provide the necessary guidance to ensure compliance with new regulations.[30]

---

[28]According to State, as long as the applicant meets the exemption criteria, the export is considered approved by the U.S. Government.

[29]National Security Decision Directive 38: Staffing at Diplomatic Missions and Their Overseas Constituent Posts and GAO, *Overseas Staffing: Rightsizing Approaches Slowly Taking Hold, But More Action Needed to Coordinate and Carry Out Efforts*, GAO-06-737 (Washington, D.C., June 30, 2006).

[30]U.S. Department of Commerce: Performance and Accountability Report, Fiscal Year 2011.

Another potential challenge with planned reform efforts includes the potential for separating criminal and administration enforcement functions currently administered by OEE. While this effort would require legislation, it could result in the transfer of OEE enforcement personnel to ICE and the administrative enforcement functions to a single licensing agency. According to OEE officials, by separating the criminal and administrative functions which are often linked in export control cases, civil fines and penalties levied in the current system may not be as actively pursued. Senior enforcement agency officials acknowledged that this and other enforcement challenges may be resolved through the Export Enforcement Coordination Center.

Conclusions

Given the wide-ranging mission of most of the agencies involved in export control enforcement, it is essential that agencies track resources expended on export control inspections, investigations, and prosecutions to assess how these resources are contributing to fulfilling their missions and are focused on the highest priorities in export control enforcement. While agencies, such as DHS and Justice, have recognized the need to better track their resources, a more comprehensive approach, including enhanced measures of effectiveness, could help these and other enforcement agencies assess workload and efficiency in making resource allocations and in determining whether changes are warranted. The creation of the Export Enforcement Coordination Center presents such an opportunity for the entire export control enforcement community. The center has the potential to become more than a co-location of enforcement agencies, but can be a conduit to more effectively manage export control resources. As the center's operation progresses, it has the opportunity to address ongoing challenges in export control enforcement, including reducing potential overlap in investigations, and help agencies to work as efficiently as possible, maximize available intelligence and agency investigative data, and measure the effectiveness of U.S. export control enforcement activities. Challenges presented by delays in license determinations can affect the inspection, investigation, and prosecution of export control cases but may be outside of the mission of the center since they primarily involve the licensing agencies. Having goals for processing license determinations can help establish transparency and accountability in the process. Given that the licensing agencies and the Exodus Command Center have not agreed to timeliness goals for responding to such requests, these agencies may benefit from collaborating to help improve the effectiveness of the process.

Recommendations for Executive Action

To better inform management and resource allocation decisions, effectively manage limited export control enforcement resources, and improve the license determination process, we are making the following four recommendations:

We recommend that the Secretary of Homeland Security and the Attorney General, as they implement efforts to track resources expended on export control enforcement activities, use such data to make resource allocation decisions.

We recommend that the Secretaries of Commerce and Homeland Security as they develop and implement qualitative measures of effectiveness, ensure that these assess progress towards their overall goal of preventing or deterring illegal exports.

We recommend that the Secretary of Homeland Security, in consultation with the departmental representatives of the Export Enforcement Coordination Center, including Commerce, Justice, State, and the Treasury

- leverage export control enforcement resources across agencies by building on existing agency efforts to track resources expended, as well as existing agency coordination at the local level;
- establish procedures to facilitate data sharing between the enforcement agencies and intelligence community to measure illicit transshipment activity; and
- develop qualitative and quantitative measures of effectiveness for the entire enforcement community to baseline and trend this data.

We recommend that the Secretaries of Commerce and State, in consultation with the Secretary of Homeland Security, the Attorney General, and other agencies as appropriate, establish agreed upon timeliness goals for responding to license determination requests considering agency resources, the level of determination, the complexity of the request, and other associated factors.

Agency Comments and Our Evaluation

We provided a draft copy of this report to Commerce, DHS, DOD, Justice, State, and Treasury for their review and comment. Commerce, DHS, Justice, and State concurred with the report's recommendations and, along with DOD, provided technical comments which we incorporated as appropriate. Treasury did not provide any comments on the report.

As multiple agencies have responsibilities for export control enforcement, several of our recommendations call for these agencies to work together to effectively manage limited export control enforcement resources and to improve the license determination process. In their comments, Commerce and State agreed to work in consultation with DHS and Justice to establish timeliness goals for license determinations. In its comments, DHS stated its intent to work with the other agencies to improve the license determination process as well as take steps to deploy its resources in the most effective and efficient manner and provided target dates for completing these actions. In particular, DHS noted that ongoing tracking efforts by CBP and ICE will be used to improve their knowledge of resources expended on export control enforcement activities and that they will periodically review this information to determine the overall direction of the export control program. Additionally, DHS stated its intent to establish a working group with other agencies to develop performance measures related to export control enforcement to help estimate the effectiveness of all associated law enforcement activity. Written comments from Commerce, DHS, and State are reprinted in appendixes II, III, and IV, respectively.

We are sending copies of this report to interested congressional committees, as well as the Secretaries of Commerce, Defense, Homeland Security, State, and Treasury as well as the Attorney General. We will also make copies available to others upon request. In addition, the report will be available at no charge on GAO's Web site at http://www.gao.gov.

If you or your staff have any questions on matters discussed in this report, please contact me at (202) 512-4841 or martinb@gao.gov. Contact points for our Offices of Congressional Relations and Public Affairs may be found on the last page of this report. GAO staff that made key contributions to this report is listed in appendix V.

Belva M. Martin
Director
Acquisition and Sourcing Management

Appendix I: Scope and Methodology

To determine how agencies allocate staff resources for export control enforcement activities, we interviewed cognizant officials and examined relevant documents such as agencies' budgets, strategic plans, memorandum, and other documentation on resources. We interviewed officials about their resources at the headquarters of Commerce, DHS, Justice, State, and the Treasury. We also discussed with DOD officials their role in providing investigative support to agencies responsible for export control enforcement. We developed and used a set of structured questions to interview each agency's resource planners to determine how they allocate resources, what information and factors they consider in resource allocation decisions, what their enforcement priorities are, whether they track resources expended on enforcement, if they had conducted an analysis of their resource need, and if they consider or leverage other agencies' resources. We obtained applicable criteria including the Office of Management and Budget Circular A-11 and departmental guidance on resource allocation and tracking. We also reviewed previous GAO and inspector general reports regarding the Government Performance and Results Act (GPRA), as amended, and resource management for enforcement programs. To determine current resource levels, we obtained geographic locations of all domestic staff conducting export control enforcement, actual expenditures on export control enforcement activities, and information on staffing levels from each agency for fiscal years 2006 through 2010. We did not independently verify the accuracy of agency information on expenditures and staffing levels obtained, but we corroborated this information with cognizant agency officials. We considered agencies' overall resources for the broad enforcement authorities and the resources allocated to export control enforcement specifically. Finally, we analyzed agencies' budget requests, expenditures, and staff hours to determine agencies current resource commitment and how agencies have allocated resources to export control enforcement activities.

To determine challenges that agencies face in investigating illicit transshipments and the potential impact of export control reform initiatives on enforcement activities, we interviewed cognizant officials, examined and analyzed relevant export control documents and statutes, and conducted sites visits both domestically and overseas. We interviewed officials about their enforcement priorities at the headquarters of Commerce, DHS, Justice, and State. We also discussed with DOD officials their role in providing license determination support to agencies responsible for export control enforcement. We developed and used a set of structured questions to interview enforcement agency officials in selected domestic and overseas locations and observed export enforcement operations at those locations that had air, land, and seaports. We selected sites to visit based on various factors, including geographical areas where all enforcement agencies were represented with a large percentage of investigative caseload; areas with a mix of defense and high-tech companies represented; ports with a high volume of trade of U.S. commodities; a large presence of aerospace, electronics, and software industries, and based on headquarters officials' recommendations on key areas of export control enforcement activities both domestically and abroad. On the basis of these factors, we visited Irvine, Long Beach, Los Angeles, Oakland, San Francisco, and San Jose, CA; Washington, D.C.; and Baltimore, MD domestically. Internationally, we interviewed United States Embassy and Consulate officials and host government authorities in Hong Kong, Singapore, and in Abu Dhabi and Dubai in the United Arab Emirates (UAE). We received briefings on the export control systems from the Hong Kong Government's Trade and Industry Department, Customs and Excise Tax Department, from Singapore's Ministry of Foreign Affairs, Singapore's Immigration and Customs Authority; as well as toured ports at these locations. We also received a briefing from the Hong Kong Customs Airport Command on air cargo and air-to-air transshipment of strategic commodities and visited the DHL Hub at the Hong Kong International Airport. In the UAE, we visited the Government of Sharjah, Department of Seaports & Customs, Hamriyah Free Zone Authority and met with the Director and Security and Safety Manager to discuss the Hamriyah Free Zone. We reviewed the findings and recommendations of past GAO reports, documentation from enforcement agencies, and interviewed U.S. government officials from these agencies as well as their field offices. We also met with several agency representatives of the Export Control Reform Task Force and reviewed recent White House press releases on the export reform initiatives. Further, we examined Federal Register notices on changing regulations related to the export control reform initiative.

We conducted this performance audit from February 2011 through March 2012, in accordance with generally accepted government auditing standards. Those standards require that we plan and perform the audit to obtain sufficient, appropriate evidence to provide a reasonable basis for our findings and conclusions based on our audit objectives. We believe that the evidence obtained provides a reasonable basis for our findings and conclusions based on our audit objectives.

Appendix II: Comments from the Department of Commerce

UNITED STATES DEPARTMENT OF COMMERCE
The Secretary of Commerce
Washington, D.C. 20230

March 14, 2012

Ms. Belva M. Martin
Director
Acquisition and Sourcing Management
Government Accountability Office (GAO)
441 G Street NW
Washington, DC 20548

Dear Ms. Martin:

Thank you for the opportunity to comment on the draft report entitled, "EXPORT CONTROLS: Proposed Reforms Create Opportunities to Address Enforcement Challenges" (GAO-12-246).

The Department of Commerce concurs with the recommendations made by the GAO to Commerce, the Department of Homeland Security, and the Department of Justice to take steps—individually and with the State and Treasury Departments through the national Export Enforcement Coordination Center—to better track, manage, and coordinate export control enforcement resources and to establish agreed-upon timelines for responding to license determination requests. I have enclosed additional detailed comments on the report.

If you need further assistance, please contact Mark Crace in the Bureau of Industry and Security's Office of Administration. Mr. Crace may be reached at (202) 482-8093 or mark.crace@bis.doc.gov.

Sincerely,

John E. Bryson

Attachments

(1) BIS comments to GAO draft report
(2) Assistant Secretary David Mills' QFR response for the hearing on "Addressing Potential Threats from Iran: Administration Perspectives on Implementing New Economic Sanctions One Year Later," October 13, 2011

Appendix III: Comments from the Department of Homeland Security

U.S. Department of Homeland Security
Washington, DC 20528

Homeland Security

March 20, 2012

Belva M. Martin
Director, Acquisition and Sourcing Management
U.S. Government Accountability Office
441 G Street, NW
Washington, DC 20548

Re: Draft Report GAO-12-246, "EXPORT CONTROLS: Proposed Reforms Create
       Opportunities to Address Enforcement Challenges"

Dear Ms. Martin:

Thank you for the opportunity to review and comment on this draft report. The U.S. Department of Homeland Security (DHS) appreciates the U.S. Government Accountability Office's (GAO's) work in planning and conducting its review and issuing this report.

DHS is pleased to note GAO's positive recognition of Departmental efforts to better track and allocate resources devoted to export control enforcement, using a risk-based approach. DHS remains committed to working with its partners, including the U.S. Departments of Commerce, Justice, State and Treasury, to further leverage our resources and improve export control enforcement activities, as appropriate.

The draft report contained four recommendations with which DHS concurs. Specifically, GAO recommended:

Recommendation 1: That the Secretary of Homeland Security and the Attorney General, as they implement efforts to track resources expended on export control enforcement activities, use such data to make resource allocation decisions.

Response: Concur. Before GAO concluded its field work, DHS began implementing efforts to address this recommendation. For example, U.S. Immigration and Customs Enforcement (ICE) is using a new strategic planning and results-based performance review process called Homeland Security Investigation (HSI) Transparency/Results/Accountability/Knowledge Sharing (TRAK), which facilitates the quantitative and qualitative analysis of available data. This process allows managers to focus on the successes and challenges unique to ICE's field offices, including resource allocation. Additionally, U.S. Customs and Border Protection (CBP) Office of Field

Operations (OFO) Outbound Enforcement Division will work to improve how they track
resources expended on export control enforcement activities. OFO will work on improving
existing processes that capture baseline officer resources expended in support of export control
activities. OFO estimates that it will complete the desired improvements by the end of CY 2012,
to have ports of entry report the resource export control data requested by GAO. The measures
derived in response to this recommendation will be reviewed periodically to determine the
overall direction of the export control program.

Recommendation 2: That the Secretaries of Commerce and Homeland Security as they develop
and implement qualitative measures of effectiveness, ensure that they assess progress towards
their overall goal of preventing or deterring illegal exports.

Response: Concur. DHS has already moved to a more robust performance measurement system
which measures the percentage of high impact/significant investigations that result in a
dismantlement or disruption of criminal organizations involved in illegal exports. ICE uses this
same system to examine the impact, effectiveness, and outcomes of counter-proliferation
investigations. Further, ICE tracks systemic vulnerabilities nationally and within its respective
field offices to prioritize its efforts. ICE HSI has also established procedures to facilitate data
sharing between the enforcement agencies and intelligence community to measure illicit
transshipment activity.

DHS will work to develop qualitative measures of effectiveness to ensure that these assess
progress towards the goal of preventing or detecting illegal exports. CBP's OFO will track the
overall number of targeted export control enforcement referrals made by officers at the ports of
entry and compare this information to the number of referrals made by officers that required
positive or negative enforcement actions. A high ratio of positive enforcement actions compared
to the total number of referrals would be indicative of success. A high ratio of negative
enforcement actions compared to the total number of referrals would indicate areas that need
improvement. The measures derived in response to this recommendation will be reviewed
periodically to determine the overall direction of the export control program.

CBP OFO personnel estimate they will be able to capture and report on export control
effectiveness measures by the end of CY 2012. The exact nature of the information, sources, and
documentation will be subject to negotiations among the agencies.

Recommendation 3: The Secretary of Homeland Security, in consultation with the
departmental representatives of the Export Enforcement Coordination Center, including
Commerce, Justice, State, and the Treasury:

   a. leverage export control enforcement resources across agencies by building on existing
      agency efforts to track resources expended, as well as existing agency coordination at
      the local level;

2

b. establish procedures to facilitate data sharing between the enforcement agencies and intelligence community to measure illicit transshipment activity; and,

c. develop qualitative and quantitative measures of effectiveness for the entire enforcement community to baseline and trend this data.

Response: Concur. DHS already has a number of initiatives that leverage resources across agencies. For example, the Export Enforcement Control Center (E2C2), led by ICE, acts as an interagency coordination center for export enforcement. In addition CBP, which operates the International Trade Data System (ITDS), is establishing a repository for all import and export data and requirements. Finally, the President's Export Control Reform Initiative is designed to bring efficiencies on a number of levels to export control. Using these initiatives as a starting point, DHS is committed to working with the U.S. Departments of Commerce, Justice, State, and Treasury to further enhance export controls and related enforcement activities.

In addition, the DHS Office of Intelligence and Analysis oversees the enterprise-wide initiatives that provide a way ahead for cross-cutting architecture of information sharing services and capabilities. The Information Sharing and Safeguarding Governance Board and its subordinate body, the Information Sharing Coordination Council, coordinate efforts to implement data sharing processes to streamline the flow of information between enforcement agencies and the intelligence community ultimately leading to more effective law enforcement.

DHS intends to establish a working group with its partners by the end of September 2012 to establish performance measures related to export enforcement that will help estimate the effectiveness of all associated law enforcement activity. The group will define measures by the end of March 2013, and implement new measures, as appropriate, by the end of June 2013.

Recommendation 4: That the Secretaries of Commerce and State, in consultation with the Secretary of Homeland Security, the Attorney General, and other agencies as appropriate, establish agreed upon timeliness goals for responding to license determination requests considering agency resources, the level of determination, the complexity of the request, and other associated factors.

Response: Concur. DHS will work with the U.S. Department of Commerce to establish agreed upon timelines for responding to license determination requests. DHS is committed to working with the Department of Commerce to use these initiatives to improve export controls, and, through the Export Enforcement Coordination Center, consulting with the Departments of Commerce, Justice, State, and Treasury to deploy our resources in the most effective and efficient way.

3

Again, thank you for the opportunity to review and comment on this draft report. The technical and sensitivity comments on the report were previously provided under separate cover. We look forward to working with you on future Homeland Security issues.

Sincerely,

Jim H. Crumpacker
Director
Departmental GAO-OIG Liaison Office

4

Appendix IV: Comments from the Department of State

United States Department of State

Chief Financial Officer

Washington, D.C. 20520

MAR 09 2012

Mr. Loren Yager
Managing Director
International Affairs and Trade
Government Accountability Office
441 G Street, N.W.
Washington, D.C. 20548-0001

Dear Mr. Yager:

We appreciate the opportunity to review your draft report, "EXPORT CONTROLS: Proposed Reforms Create Opportunities to Address Enforcement Challenges," GAO Job Code 120966.

The enclosed Department of State comments are provided for incorporation with this letter as an appendix to the final report.

If you have any questions concerning this response, please contact Steven Rice, Deputy Director, Bureau of Political-Military Affairs at (202) 663-2803.

Sincerely,

James L. Millette

cc: GAO – Belva Martin
      PM– Andrew J. Shapiro
      State/OIG – Evelyn Klemstine

Department of State Comments on GAO Draft Report

**EXPORT CONTROLS: Proposed Reforms Create Opportunities to Address
Enforcement Challenges**
GAO-12-246, Job Code 120966

Thank you for the opportunity to comment on your draft report entitled, *"Export
Controls: Proposed Reforms Create Opportunities to Address Enforcement
Challenges."* With respect to the fourth recommendation GAO made in the draft
report, the Department of State agrees with the recommendation and will work in
consultation with the Departments of Homeland Security and Justice to establish
timeliness goals for license determinations. These goals will reflect our agency
resources, the complexity of the request and other factors.

Appendix V: GAO Contact and Staff Acknowledgments

GAO Contact	Belva Martin, (202) 512-4841 or martinb@gao.gov.
Staff Acknowledgments	In addition to the contact names above, John Neumann, Assistant Director; Lisa Gardner; Desiree Cunningham; Jungjin Park; Marie Ahearn; Roxanna Sun; Robert Swierczek; and Hai Tran made key contributions to this report.

GAO's Mission	The Government Accountability Office, the audit, evaluation, and investigative arm of Congress, exists to support Congress in meeting its constitutional responsibilities and to help improve the performance and accountability of the federal government for the American people. GAO examines the use of public funds; evaluates federal programs and policies; and provides analyses, recommendations, and other assistance to help Congress make informed oversight, policy, and funding decisions. GAO's commitment to good government is reflected in its core values of accountability, integrity, and reliability.
Obtaining Copies of GAO Reports and Testimony	The fastest and easiest way to obtain copies of GAO documents at no cost is through GAO's website (www.gao.gov). Each weekday afternoon, GAO posts on its website newly released reports, testimony, and correspondence. To have GAO e-mail you a list of newly posted products, go to www.gao.gov and select "E-mail Updates."
Order by Phone	The price of each GAO publication reflects GAO's actual cost of production and distribution and depends on the number of pages in the publication and whether the publication is printed in color or black and white. Pricing and ordering information is posted on GAO's website, http://www.gao.gov/ordering.htm. Place orders by calling (202) 512-6000, toll free (866) 801-7077, or TDD (202) 512-2537. Orders may be paid for using American Express, Discover Card, MasterCard, Visa, check, or money order. Call for additional information.
Connect with GAO	Connect with GAO on Facebook, Flickr, Twitter, and YouTube. Subscribe to our RSS Feeds or E-mail Updates. Listen to our Podcasts. Visit GAO on the web at www.gao.gov.
To Report Fraud, Waste, and Abuse in Federal Programs	Contact: Website: www.gao.gov/fraudnet/fraudnet.htm E-mail: fraudnet@gao.gov Automated answering system: (800) 424-5454 or (202) 512-7470
Congressional Relations	Katherine Siggerud, Managing Director, siggerudk@gao.gov, (202) 512-4400, U.S. Government Accountability Office, 441 G Street NW, Room 7125, Washington, DC 20548
Public Affairs	Chuck Young, Managing Director, youngc1@gao.gov, (202) 512-4800 U.S. Government Accountability Office, 441 G Street NW, Room 7149 Washington, DC 20548

Please Print on Recycled Paper.

www.ingramcontent.com/pod-product-compliance
Lightning Source LLC
Chambersburg PA
CBHW080917290526
45795CB00007BA/2551

* 9 7 8 1 4 9 2 2 8 9 1 5 9 *